Strange Creatures
and Other Poems

Marvin Druger

January 22, 2005

*To Morgan —
With Warmest Best
Wishes of the author*

D R U G E R   B Y   T H E   L A K E

Marvin Druger

First Edition 2004
04 05 06 07 08 09   7 6 5 4 3 2 1

Library of Congress Cataloging-in-Publication Data
available upon request.
ISBN 0-9762819-0-2

Manufactured in the United States of America

Strange Creatures and Other Poems

Dedicated to my wife Pat

for her love and patience

and to my grandchildren

Keith, Lindsey, Aaron, Joshua, and Rachel

for their inspiration

CoNTeNTS

BeGiNNiNgs

StraNge ThiNgs

PeoPLe and BEHavioR

FooD

LoVe and CaRing

NatuRe

You Can WriTe PoeMs, Too

PrEfaCe

Every second of our lives, we experience something new. Even a repetition of the same experience is not exactly the same. We learn from everything that we do, and everything that we do becomes part of what we are. This book reflects on our everyday experiences and our environments. Each poem carries a thoughtful message about life and the world around us. Sometimes, life is sad; sometimes it is fun; sometimes, it is ridiculous. These different moods and observations appear in the poems. I hope that these poems will encourage readers to write their own poems. "If I can do it, anyone can!"

So, read, experience and enjoy *Strange Creatures and Other Poems.*

Marvin Druger
Syracuse University

AcKNOWLedGMENTS

This book is the fulfillment of a dream that started several years ago while I was reading a childrens' book to my granddaughter, Lindsey. The book was terrible, yet it was, indeed, a published book. I thought that I could do better, so I started writing poems about life. I want to thank my grandchildren (Keith, Lindsey, Aaron, Joshua, and Rachel) for their enthusiastic response to the poems and for listening to me read them many times.

The expert assistance of Mary Peterson Moore, Design and Production Manager at the Syracuse University Press is deeply appreciated. Thanks to Fred Wellner for scanning the illustrations, and Victoria Lane and Mike Rankin for being a receptive audience for my jokes and stories. I also want to thank Kathleen Bradley, Elena De Vita, Lisa Kuerbis and the Syracuse University Bookstore staff for their advice, encouragement and for arranging poetry readings at the Bookstore. I thank Barbara J. Carns for proofreading the manuscript. I appreciate the encouraging support of Michele McFee, Biology 121–123 Course Coordinator, and Mary Selden Evans, Executive Editor, Syracuse University Press. The photo of the "modern human" was taken by Stephen Sartori, Syracuse University photographer. The caricature on the front cover is the product of John P. Norton, illustrator and cartoonist.

Finally, I want to thank my wife, Patricia, for her excellent advice, for technical preparation of the manuscript, for tolerating many readings of the poems, and for accepting me for what I am for more than 47 years of love and marriage.

BEGINNINGS

A Mystery

A mystery is something
That we don't know much about,
It tells us there's a puzzle
That we need to figure out.

What's in this book's a mystery,
But I'll give you a clue,
There are poems that make you think
About the things you do.

But the only way to really know
What the poems have to say,
Is to turn the page and read them,
And have a happy day.

The Play of Life

The play is ready to begin,
The audience is here,
Everyone is excited,
The starting time is near.

What is the play about
That so many came to see?
Is it something sad?
Or is it comedy?

The actors tell us
What we want to know,
Poems about life
Are what make the show.

Arrows

Arrows point the way to go,
The path is always clear,
Arrows tell us how to get
From here to anywhere.

I found an arrow in this book,
It's right here just below,
I couldn't think of why it's here,
But now I think I know.

The arrow points to the right,
So you should go that way,
And keep on turning every page
And read more poems each day.

Then you will have some thoughts
That you've never had before,
And after reading all the poems,
I'll bet you'll ask for more.

READ ON . . .

Time Marches On

Clocks are made to tell the time
And what they tell is true,
Times moves on with no regard
To anything we do.

When I'm very happy
I'd like the time to last,
And when I'm sad and gloomy
I want time to go fast.

But even if I break the clock
And throw its parts away,
Time will still move on
And bring another day.

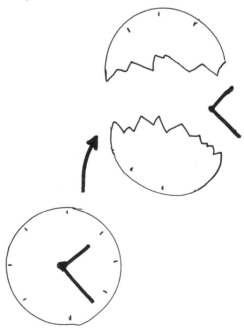

Saving Time

People like to save
Many different things,
Pennies, stamps and bottles,
Comic books and rings.

But I save something else,
That's very hard to do,
What I save is TIME,
And you can do this too.

Do everything much faster,
You use less time that way,
And with the time that's saved,
Enjoy more of the day.

More Time

Nobody has time to spare,
Time is quick to disappear,
But I can make the time return,
And this is something you can learn.

My secret is an hourglass,
It tells me how the time will pass,
The sand runs down as time goes by
And fills the bottom very high.

And then I turn it all around,
And that's the way more time is found.

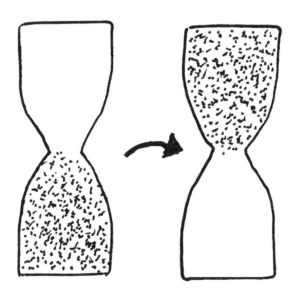

Procrastinate

A big word is "procrastinate,"
It means that everything is late,
Whatever I must do each day,
"Procrastinate" means I delay.

Though I intend to finish fast,
What is first is finished last,
I can't seem to change my fate,
Which seems to be "Procrastinate."

What's best that I might do I've heard,
Is still delay, but change the word.

Today

Today I plan to have some fun,
I'll dance and jump
And play and run,
Then I'll eat my favorite treat
And settle in my armchair seat.

I'll read the book I like so well,
The one with happy tales to tell,
But before the day will end
I'll meet with you, my favorite friend,

And one thing more that I will do,
I'll hug you and you'll hug me too,
Then at night I'll go to bed
With happy thoughts inside my head,

The day was long but full of fun,
And now to sleep, the day is done,
Tomorrow is another one.

StrANgE ThINgs

Strange Creatures

An elephant is big and strong,
It's ears are large, it's nose is long,
I laugh to see it's funny face,
Its body seems so out of place.

But then I think how it would be,
If the elephant studied me,
My face is thin, my body's tall,
My head has hair, my nose is small.

The elephant would laugh to see
How strange I really seem to be.

Reality

Are we really what we see?
Are you you?
And am I me?
And is she she?
And is he he?
Are we all that we can be?

Absolutely Relative

How thin is thin?
How tall is tall?
How short is short?
How small is small?

The only thing we seem to know
Is if you're small, then you may grow,
Or if you're thin, you may get fat,
But we can't tell much more than that.

'Cause tall and small are relative,
And so are short and thin,
What they mean depends upon
The place where you begin.

Gravity

I jumped up high into the air
And asked, "What am I doing here?"
Will I keep going to the top?
Or will I ever have to stop?

Soon I stop my upward flight
And wonder if I'm going right?
I stop up there and look around,
And then I drop down to the ground.

How nice it was to be so high,
For just an instant I could fly.
I tried so hard to float in air,
But nothing seemed to keep me there.

Some other time, I know not when,
I think I'll try it once again.

Different Tears

I cry when I'm happy,
I cry when I'm sad,
I cry when I'm lonely,
I cry when I'm mad.

The tears from my eyes
Run straight down my face,
They drip on my clothes,
They're all over the place.

When tears start to flow
I'll catch them some day
To see if they differ
In some magic way.

For maybe the tears
When I'm happy or sad
Are different from tears
When I'm lonely or mad?

Toys

Toys can be most anything,
A doll, a car, a piece of string,
Toys are with us every day,
They are the things with which we play.

Sometimes it's just fun to see
How many things a toy can be,
A box can become a house,
A toothbrush can become a mouse,
A feather can become a bird,
Nonsense can become a word.

Our minds can make an object be
Whatever we would like to see,
So we should never have to fear,
For toys go with us everywhere,
Our mind decides what is a toy,
And makes toys things that we enjoy.

A Whisper

A whisper traveled though the air,
I strained my ears to hear it,
But the message that I heard
Was not heard when I got near it.

I wondered how a whisper
Could so quickly disappear,
The wind had blown the whisper
To another place somewhere.

And somewhere someone listened
To a whispered mystery,
The words made someone laugh,
But that someone was not me.

I tried my best to catch it,
I followed it around,
But when I finally reached it
It no longer was a sound.

So, please speak loud and clear,
Let your words ring out,
Then I won't have to wonder
What your message is about.

Foosingers

You've seen a triangle, circle and square,
A rectangle, pentagon, cube and a sphere,
But I'll bet that you have never seen
A foosinger shaped liked an alakazeen.

An alakazeen is such a strange shape
That it makes a foosinger look like a gazape.
Gazapes are long and they're circular too,
They twist on themselves like an alakazoo.

So, alakazeens, alakazoos and gazapes
Make foosingers look like a large bunch of grapes.
And so when a foosinger comes into view,
You'll know that its shape
Is something brand new.

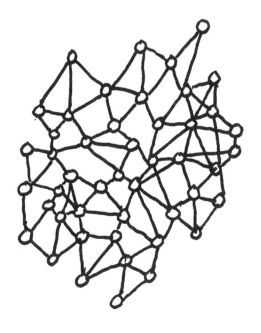

East to West

As I travel East to West
The hours start to change,
Getting there before I leave
Is really rather strange.

It seems the day gets longer
As I travel with the sun,
I leave the East at lunchtime
And eat breakfast when I'm done.

If I keep on going West,
Will I ever see the night?
Or will daylight be forever
And keep nighttime out of sight?

I want to know the answer
So I'll keep on going West,
If I find a spot of nighttime
I'll stop right there—and rest.

Soft and White

It was trapped inside a box,
But I would set it free,
I tugged it very hard,
'Til it popped right out at me.

It looked just like a cloud,
It was soft and white,
It rested in my hand,
It was a pretty sight.

I held it to my face,
It had an odor like a rose,
But when I tried to smell it,
It rose up and blew my nose.

My Shadow

I saw my little shadow,
And said,"How do you do?"
I looked for you last night,
But there was no sign of you.

Now it is the morning
And with the rising sun,
You appear from nowhere
And grow to be someone.

You follow me around
And stick to me like glue,
But when the sun is overhead
You disappear from view.

Then in the afternoon
Again you can be seen,
And I begin to wonder
What all this can mean?

When I know the answer
I will let you know,
But so far, it's a puzzle
As to how you come and go.

Upside Down

There is a land . . .
Where good is bad
And up is down
And sad is glad.

Where push is pull
And out is in
And loose is tight
And fat is thin.

Where north is south
And east is west
Where cold is hot
And worst is best.

Where lost is found
And white is black
And work is play
And front is back.

If I can ever
Pass that way,
I'll laugh and cry
All night and day.

Smart Computers

Computers are so smart
In everything they do,
You simply push some buttons,
And they bring the world to you.

Computers know most everything,
They're amazing in that way,
They give us lots of knowledge,
And play games with us each day.

I wonder how computers work?
How did they get so smart?
Do computers have a brain?
Do computers have a heart?

How do they think so fast?
Why do they click and whirl?
'Cause inside each computer
There's a clever little girl.

People and Behavior

Tinyness

If I was tiny, I'd be scared
Of people big and tall,
I'd try to find a hiding place
And hide away from all.

But when I start to think of it,
Being small is not so bad,
It doesn't take much space,
So I shouldn't be so sad.

For tiny as my size may be,
I've lots of personality,
So, even though my size is small,
In lots of ways, I'm big and tall.

Lazy Lee

Lazy Lee just liked to rest,
She sat around all day,
Whenever there were things to do,
She looked the other way.

Then one day an earthquake came,
It shook her where she sat,
One eye opened lazily,
She whispered, "What was that?"

The buildings shook and fell,
Trees crashed to the ground,
Bricks and wood and glass
Were scattered all around.

But Lazy Lee just yawned,
She did not have a care,
The world around was crumbling,
While she rested in her chair.

Finally, came the silence,
The earthquake now was gone,
But Lazy Lee still rested,
Never knowing what went on.

Lazy Lee missed all of life,
The worst things and the best,
Was it wise for Lazy Lee
To only sit and rest?

You Are Special

People are so different,
No two are quite the same,
Even twins are different
And have a different name.

So, it's really nice to know
That no matter what you do,
You are very special
And you are important too.

My Turtle Shell

Turtles are so interesting,
Their movements are so slow,
They have a heavy shell
That they carry where they go.

Whenever trouble comes their way,
They hide inside their shell,
No matter what the trouble is,
They hide from it quite well.

I wish I had a magic shell
To carry at my side,
Whenever trouble comes along,
I'll crawl inside and hide.

My magic shell is in my mind,
I think bad thoughts away,
And just like turtles in their shell,
I'm happy every day.

Words

Words are sort of fun to use,
They also can be strange,
Rambunctious, rambling, elevate,
Ambitious, stress, arrange.

Words are an important way
To tell the way we feel,
They help us tell to others
What's fantasy or real.

Words can act as weapons,
They can hurt and sting,
They can make you laugh or cry,
They say most anything.

So think before you speak,
Let words come from your brain,
For once they've left your mouth,
You can't take them back again.

Walking

When I travel very far,
I can go by bus or car,
I can go by boat or train,
I can even take a plane.

I can go most anywhere,
And find a way for getting there,
But there's one way that I like the best,
It's much more fun than all the rest.

Although this way is not too quick,
It's the one I'm quick to pick,
For I can stop and laugh and talk,
And that's why I would choose to walk.

There are many people I can meet,
When I travel with my feet,
The distances are not so great
When I don't care if I am late,
I see the sights and make good friends,
And walk until my journey ends.

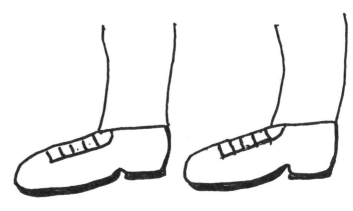

Halloween

The night darkens
And creatures of all colors
Sizes and shapes emerge,
New species never ever seen,
Except at Halloween.

All these creatures eat
Only what is sweet,
Candy, gum and sugar corn
Is what they eat,
Their cries ring out in the night,
"Trick or treat!"

I caught one ghostlike creature
Early on that night,
It appeared upon my doorstep
And gave me quite a fright.

I picked it up and tickled it,
It laughed a laugh of joy,
Then magically it changed itself
Into a little boy.

So, I'm no longer frightened
By creatures fierce and mean,
I simply smile and say to them . . .
"HAPPY HALLOWEEN!"

Counting Sheep

When I couldn't fall asleep,
I was told to count some sheep,
I closed my eyes and counted four,
But that woke me up even more.
Then I tried to count to ten,
The sheep were in my mind again.

Soon sleep came rushing to my head,
I dreamt that sheep were in my bed.
I liked the warmth of fuzzy wool,
To sleep with sheep was really cool.

The sheep were gone when I awoke,
I thought the whole thing was a joke,
But then I found some woolly hair,
I guess the sheep were really there.

So when I sleep I count to ten,
And hope the sheep come back again.

Fly Thoughts

A little fly landed nearby,
It cleaned its little wing,
It rubbed its legs together
And seemed pleased with everything.

When it saw that I was there,
It quickly flew away,
It landed on the ceiling
And was upside down that way.

I stared at it,
It stared at me,
But not a word was said,
And both of us would wonder
What was in the other's head.

The fly was thinking,
"Will he smash me?
Will he try to kill?"
But I was thinking,
"How can a fly be standing
Upside down and be so still?"

The fly decided not to wait
To see what I would do,
It dropped quickly from the ceiling
And flew far out of view.

The lesson that this taught me
Is that we can't always tell
What someone else is thinking,
Though we think we know quite well.

So when we deal with others,
It's important that we try
To think the thoughts that they think
And to ask the reasons why.

Need

Sometimes I think it's funny
That folks think it's great
To have lots of money.

Is it good to have wealth?
Is it bad to be poor?

If I have what I need
Do I need any more?

The Beautiful Beast

I've heard of Beauty and the Beast,
It gave me quite a fright,
The Beast was very ugly,
And he howled and screamed all night.

But Beauty tamed the savage Beast,
She soothed his evil mind,
She laughed and played
And joked with him,
'Til he became quite kind.

He stopped his fits
And laughed with her,
That now became his duty,
And after all was said and done,
The Beast became a Beauty.

A Lesson in Life

A small boy in Morocco
Weaving a rug on a loom,
My family watching,
The guide's proclamation,
"See, you're lucky,
You don't have to be
Like him!"

My son: high school, college,
A career, involvements,
Success and happiness,
The young rug weaver:
Poverty, suffering
And early death.

Where is equality of opportunity
And justice?
A lesson in life,
Don't waste an opportunity
That millions of others
Will never have.

My Future

When I think about my future
I don't know what I'll be,
But if I do my best
I can make much more of me.

My Greatness

Nobody says I'm great,
So I have to tell them all
That I'm the greatest person
That anyone can recall.

Why do I boast so much,
Much more than someone should?
'Cause if I didn't praise myself,
No other person would.

But someone who is truly great
Has no need to say,
'Cause others do that job
In an enthusiastic way.

Please and Thank You

Please and thank you
Are words I like to hear,
They represent politeness
That is welcome everywhere.

But sometimes we forget
To say what is polite,
We act in a rude manner
And don't say what is right.

Then we have to be reminded
Our behavior was not proper,
When my sister says rude words,
I try my best to stop her.

Foggy

When I sleep,
I sleep like a log,
When I'm awake,
I'm in a fog.

My Family

Being in a family
Is the nicest place to be,
There's a lot of talk to share
And food and fun are always there,
Brother, sister, mom and dad,
Are the ones that make me glad.

Sometimes things don't go quite right
And there may be a family fight,
But very soon after the tears
The thought of fighting disappears,
And angry feelings we had then
Are lost in family love again.

Music

Music is a pleasant sound,
That travels everywhere,
It tickles the typanum
As it penetrates the ear.

It travels to the brain
Where it lingers for awhile,
Then it goes straight to my body
And it makes my body smile.

So, if I want to feel happy
I know just what to do,
I simply hum a happy tune,
Doodle, doo, de, doo.

One Penny

A little girl dropped me
Right at her feet,
I rolled from her pocket
Right onto the street.

I lay on the sidewalk
As people walked by,
They chose to ignore me
And I think I know why.

They don't seem to know
'Though I'm just a penny,
If they pick us all up
We add up to many.

A Bearded Man

I saw a bearded man
Whose face was lost in hair,
I tried to figure out
What was hidden there.

All that I could see
Was his mouth and nose and eyes,
The face behind the beard
Could be a big surprise.

His chin could be quite small,
And it may well have a dimple,
Perhaps there is a scar,
Or maybe there's a pimple.

His eyes looked right at me,
His lips gave me a smile,
He knew what I was thinking,
"Was he the latest style?"

The man laughed at my stare,
He raised his hand to wave,
His friendly, happy manner
Made me never want to shave.

Age and Beauty

Age and beauty go together,
That's what people say,
They say it's better to be young,
But we age every day.

As we age our wisdom grows
And we grow more mature,
We become more beautiful
Than we ever were before.

 So be sure to celebrate
That you've lived another year,
And keep on gaining wisdom
And have a HAPPY BIRTHDAY, dear.

Older People

Many people who are old
Seem silly in their ways,
They always seem to talk
About the good old days.

They talk about the past,
And how grand it used to be,
They always try to tell us
What they've stored in memory.

To them it makes no difference
That many things are past,
Because when we get older
We want the past to last.

Noses

Noses are big,
Noses are small,
They come in all shapes,
But the best thing of all,
Is though they look different,
We know very well,
That wherever they go
Noses know how to smell.

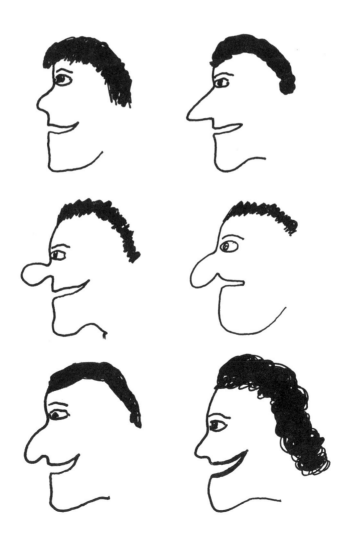

Work and Play

I do work most every day,
It's sometimes not much fun,
I try to do my best
To get lots of it done.

I grow tired every night
From work done in the day,
I go to sleep and in my dreams,
I dream that work is play.

When I awake I realize
That work is not so bad,
And if I think of work as play,
I change from sad to glad.

So now when I have work to do
It doesn't bother me,
I see my work as lots of fun
And I do it cheerfully.

Jogging

Jogging is a lot of fun,
I can think while I run.
At the start I'm breathing fast,
But heavy breathing does not last.

Soon I feel like a machine,
I float along and view each scene,
My feet move quickly on the ground,
While in mind new thoughts are found,
Bur the best part of the jogging hour
Is when I stop . . .

And take a shower.

The Grump

I am a grump.
I'm nasty and mean,
I'm the grumpiest grump
That's ever been seen.

When someone says "yes,"
I always say "no,"
I'm a negative grump
Wherever I go.

I complain about everything,
Nothing is right,
I make people miserable,
That's my delight.

Someone suggested
That I try to smile,
I think I will try
But it may take awhile.

I'll stretch my lips
In an upward direction,
I'll practice a smile
'Til it reaches perfection.

My face looks so strange,
My lips now are curled,
My teeth are exposed,
As I smile at the world.

Hey, I never knew
That a smile feels so good,
I'm losing my grumps,
They told me I would.

My whole life is changed now,
I've learned a new style,
I'm no longer a grump,
'Cause I know how to smile.

A Teacher's Farewell

Nobody likes to say "goodbye,"
We would rather just say "hi,"
But "goodbye" means we go away,
Even though I'd rather stay.

Teaching you was lots of fun,
I'm sorry that the class is done,
We had so many special days
And learned so much so many ways.

The lessons learned should strengthen you
And help you do all that you do,
I hope what you have learned from me
Will help you be all you can be.

A Computer Nerd

A computer is my friend
We do everything together
I spend all my time with it,
No matter what the weather.

I play many games,
I find out many things,
I learn about the world,
About bugs and worms and kings.

I sit and punch the keys,
That's all I ever do
My mom says I should exercise,
She says "It's good for you."

But when I think of exercise
I lie down in my bed,
Until the thought is gone
And computers fill my head.

I never go outside,
I know it seems absurd,
Every minute of the day,
I'm a computer Nerd.

FOOD

Grapes

I bought a bunch of grapes,
The price was very low,
I wondered how they tasted,
There was one way I could know.

I put one in my mouth,
Its skin was green and slick,
I crunched it with my teeth,
And chewed it up real quick.

A burst of flavor filled my mouth,
The taste was really good,
I like the grapes so well
That I ate more than I should.

So now my stomach's full,
I can't eat any more,
If you mention grapes to me,
I'll throw up on the floor.

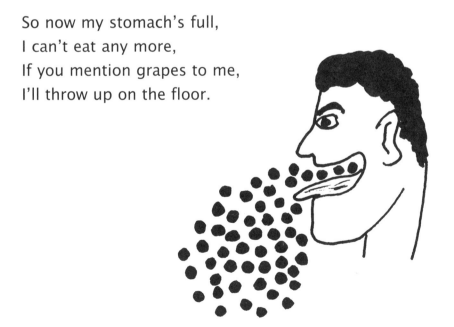

Pizza

I have a special treat for you,
A pizza that is truly new,
Use tomato paste and cheese,
And whatever else you please.

Add some nuts and macaroni,
Then throw in some beef baloney.
Sprinkle it with lots of candy,
Use whatever else is handy.

Pickles are a tasty treat,
They make the pizza good to eat,
Then add some tangerines
And cover them with chocolate beans.

Then soak it all in sweetened four
And bake the mix for just an hour,
When the pizza's finally done,
Give a piece to everyone.

Eating this will make them smile,
And they'll be in the bathroom for awhile.

Chips

Potato chips are great to eat,
They are now my favorite treat,
I like the salty taste
And I like they way they crunch,
I eat them as a snack
And I eat them with my lunch.

I try not to eat too many,
I really try my best,
But after I eat one,
I must eat all the rest.

Mom hides the potato chips
On a high shelf in the hall,
I know the secret hiding place
But I am not that tall.

So, I can't reach the chips
And best that I can do,
Is dream I eat potato chips
And hope my dream comes true.

Special Sandwich

I start with toasted bread,
And then I add some meat,
Ham, turkey and salami
Are what I like to eat.

Then I put on lettuce,
And add a slice of cheese,
This sandwich seems so good,
But it needs much more please.

So, I add a bit of honey,
And peanut butter too,
With mayonnaise and mustard,
The sandwich tastes like glue.

But it's a special sandwich
That shouldn't go to waste,
So chew and swallow quickly
To avoid its special taste.

Too Fat

I ate a lot of food
And I became too fat,
I grew too big all over,
Especially where I sat.

I can't imagine how
I grew fatter than a cow,
So one day I decided
To lose a lot of weight,
I went on a strict diet
And I started to feel great.

I exercised each day
And much to my surprise,
I lost a lot of pounds
And became a smaller size.

If you get fat like I did
And want to lose weight too,
Exercise and eating less
Can do the job for you.

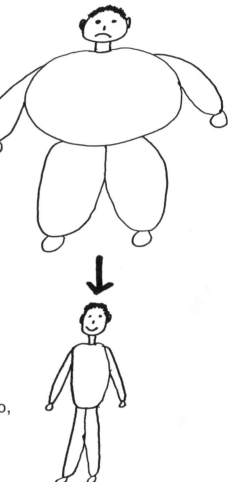

Sweet Dreams

When I go to sleep at night
I never seem to know
Where my dreams will take me
And what wonders they will show.

Last night I was in candy land,
The first time I've been there,
Lollipops and candy bars
Could be found everywhere.

Chocolate fudge and Tootsie Rolls,
Smarties, Skittles, too,
Any candy you could want
Was there for me and you.

I ate a Gummi Teddy Bear,
And licked a lollipop,
I ate and ate and ate and ate,
I couldn't seem to stop.

My stomach got so full
That I started to feel sick,
But just then I awoke,
And I woke up very quick.

My stomach pain was gone,
No candy was in sight,
The happy trip to candy land
Had passed by in the night.

But I enjoyed that dream,
It was really fun,
I hope that tomorrow's sleep
Will bring another one.

The Growling Stomach

I hear my stomach growl,
It sounds just like a bear,
I cannot figure out
What is happening there.

I eat a bit of food,
This makes the growling stop,
The animal in my stomach,
Must like the food a lot.

So whenever in my stomach
It sounds like there's a riot,
I simply eat a bagel
And it keeps the animal quiet.

Ice is Nice

My drink was warm, it tasted bad,
The worst drink that I've ever had,
Then I had some good advice,
A friend told me to add some ice.

So I put ice cubes in my drink,
They floated there and did not sink,
I watched the ice cubes disappear,
They went away, I know not where.

Soon the cubes were fully gone,
But their coldness lingered on,
Now the drink was really good,
It tasted like a good drink should.

The ice cubes never became old,
They disappeared, but left the cold,
I thanked my friend for good advice,
'Cause now I know that ice is nice.

Sharing a Bagel

We both wanted a bagel,
But there was only one,
I thought of how to share it,
And it was lots of fun.

I said we should pretend
That the bagel was a roll,
I tore it right in half
And gave my friend the hole.

LoVe and CaRiNG

What Love Means

One day while walking down the street
A little girl I did meet,
She said that she wanted to find
How the word "love" might be defined.

The meaning was inside my head
And I was pleased with what I said:
"Love" is when I want to do
Less for me, and more for you.

My Teddy

I love my little teddy bear,
He is my favorite friend,
I go to sleep with him each night,
On that you can depend.

Sometimes, I awaken him
In the middle of the night,
I tell him funny stories
And I giggle with delight.

I love my little teddy bear,
I take him every place,
He feels so warm and cuddly
When I hug him to my face.

But I know when I am older,
And other interests grow,
The teddy I once knew
Won't be the teddy that I know.

Now he is so dear to me,
But when I'm more mature,
The teddy of my childhood
Will be gone forevermore.

But no matter what my age,
And no matter where I'll be,
I'll always have my teddy
As a happy memory.

Good night teddy . . .
Wherever you are.

My Secret Friend

When I go to sleep each night
I meet a secret friend,
I tell it all my cares
As the day comes to an end.

I press my cheek against it
And I hold it very tight,
I whisper that "I love you,"
And then turn out the light.

I sleep a peaceful sleep
And feel so warm and snug,
All because my "blankie"
Gives me a great big hug.

73

The Tree

A tree that stands so straight and high
Spreads its branches toward the sky,
The branches are a lovely sight,
The leaves on them are green and bright.

The tree that stands above the ground
Has hidden roots that can be found,
Below the earth we cannot see
The roots that help support the tree.

They give it strength and water too,
We cannot see all that they do,
And just as roots support the tree,
My family gives support to me.

My Secret

I had a little secret
Hidden in my mind,
It stayed inside my head
And was very hard to find.

One day my little secret
Caused a bit of pain,
As it squeezed out of my head
And departed from my brain.

It reached my lips
And leaped outside
Right into the air,
My little secret now was out
For everyone to hear.

What was this little secret
Now every person knew?
That precious little secret was that

I
LOVE
U

Love and Laugh

I try to laugh my way through life
But when I'm feeling sad,
I have a way to smile again
And change the sad to glad.

Making joy return
Is an easy thing to do,
I simply fill my mind
With loving thoughts of you.

When you are in my mind,
You fill up all the space,
Sad thoughts cannot fit
And they go some other place.

Then I'm happy once again,
It happens very fast,
Just the thought that I love you
Puts sadness in the past . . .

And makes my laughter last.

Darkness and Light

The room was dark,
There was no light,
Yet this darkness
Was not night.

My thoughts were sad,
They made life dark,
My life was empty,
There was no spark.

Suddenly the room lit up,
Happiness had come,
The brilliance was amazing
And I knew where it was from.

She lit up the room,
Her beauty was so bright,
Her laugh made me so happy
It removed the black of night.

So whenever darkness comes
I think of my dear one,
And then the light bulbs glow
And all of life is fun.

Booky and Cooky

Booky Tooky once met Cooky,
They made a handsome pair,
Booky Tooky married Cooky
And after just a year,
Booky Tooky had a baby,
A cuddly little boy,
They had to find a name for him,
A name he would enjoy,
Finally, they chose a name,
They named him after Booky,
The baby's name that Booky chose
Was Booky Tooky Shnooky.

A Kinder, Better Place

One day I saw an old man
Walking down the street,
He had a cane and limped along
And rags were on his feet.

I stopped to ask him why
His feet appeared so funny,
He answered me and said,
"Because I have no money."

"I can help," I said,
"For I have hidden treasure,
I can buy some shoes for you,
It will be my pleasure."

The old man seemed surprised and said,
"But why should you help me?
I'm just a poor old man
With no shoes, as you can see?"

"That's why I want to help you,
When I see someone poor,
I think about my own wealth
And that I have so much more."

"So I want to share my wealth
With those who are in need.
It makes me feel so good
To do a thoughtful deed."

I wish that others wanted
To help the human race,
If that were true the world
Would be a kinder, better place.

Sharing Wealth

If I had lots of money,
I'd travel far and near,
I'd visit Greece and Spain,
I'd go most everywhere.

In every place I'd stay awhile
And I would live in wealthy style,
I'd buy the finest clothes and such
And I would never lack for much.

But would it make me feel so good,
To have more than one person should?
The world has many mouths to feed
And I'll have much more than I need.

So, I'll stop spending more and more,
I'll give my money to the poor,
And though my money would depart,
My wealth would be within my heart.

Organic Love

I love you with all my heart,
My kidneys love you too,
My lungs are crazy 'bout you,
They love everything you do.

I love you so madly
That sometimes I will shiver,
Every organ starts to shake,
Especially my liver.

My intestine fills with gas,
My stomach starts to churn,
My muscles start contracting,
My appendix starts to burn.

My heart beats very rapidly
And keeps the bloodstream flowing,
All my organs are excited
As my love for you keeps growing.

Two Old Horses

Two old horses in the field,
Both of them were white,
They rubbed against each other
And whinnied in delight.

They shared the field together,
They had lots of grass and space,
They were happy older horses
Who lived at their own pace.

I went to see them yesterday,
And much to my surprise
Only one white horse was there,
I could not believe my eyes.

"What happened to your friend?" I asked,
"Where did your partner go?"
The old horse stared at me,
She seemed to think I'd know
That her partner left this world,
That he left her all alone,
That her happiness had gone,
That her world had turned to stone.

But she was brave and strong,
She overcame her sadness,
She thought about the pleasant past
And sadness turned to gladness.

The happy memories of him
Brought her joy and laughter,
And even though she missed him,
She lived happily ever after.

Sharing

I visited the zoo one day
And saw a funny sight,
Two elephants were side-by-side
And almost had a fight.

One elephant was eating hay,
The other wanted it,
The first one took the hay away
And would not share a bit.

People can be selfish too
And never want to share,
Even if they have enough
They don't seem to care.

We hope that they will change,
But that's very hard to do,
Selfish people do exist,
But don't let one be you.

Blue is You

Your hair is blue
Your face is too
I have no clue
Why all of you
Is colored blue.

I know it's true
That blue is you
From every view
There's only blue.

What I must do
To make you new
Is color your head
And make it red.

Color me Blue

Color me Red

Nature

The Spider

The spider made its web,
It was a pretty sight,
The silky threads were hard to see,
Especially at night.

I flew right toward my home
That was behind the tree,
I didn't see the spider's web
Until it had trapped me.

I hit against the threads
And my body stuck right there,
I struggled to get free
But the web seemed everywhere.

My struggle gave the signal
And then out came the spider,
And before I knew what happened
I ended up inside her.

A Green Plant

I wish I were a green plant,
I would stand tall every day,
I would dance in pleasant breezes
And have lots of fun that way.

I would make pretty flowers
And spread my seeds around,
I would soak in happy showers
And grow roots underground.

But the best thing I would do,
I would do just in the sun,
I'd do photosynthesis
And make food for everyone.

The Lonely Flower

The beautiful flower was all by itself,
Its colors were yellow and white,
It sparkled in the sunshine,
It was truly a glorious sight.

But this flower was all alone
There were no others near,
The beautiful little flower
Had loneliness to fear.

Then one day some seeds
Dropped onto the ground,
They soon grew into plants,
And more flowers could be found.

So now our flower is happy,
It has new pretty friends,
Oneness grew to manyness,
That's how our story ends.

The Fallen Leaf

I saw a yellow leaf
Hanging on a tree,
The leaf remembers well
How green it used to be.

The wind blows briskly
And the leaf begins to drop,
It joins other yellow leaves
Gently falling from the top.

The yellow leaf seems sad
As it softly hits the ground,
It wants to find its youth,
But no greenness can be found.

The yellow leaf knows well
That it has a sorry fate,
It will disappear
While the naked tree will wait
Until the breath of Springtime
Once again is here.

Then tiny buds will blossom
And new green leaves will appear.

Rainbow

The colors of a rainbow
Seem so bright and clear,
Red and yellow, green and blue
Are curved up in the air.

When the rain departs,
And clouds move out of sight,
The colors of the rainbow
Mix together and look white.

When clouds return again
And raindrops start to fall,
The colors of the rainbow
Can again be seen by all.

Birds, Cats and Squirrels

I have a bird house in my yard,
I watch it every day,
The birds fly in and eat the seeds
And then they fly away.

Before the birds go near the seeds
They always look around,
They seem to want to see
If danger can be found.

One day a cat was in my yard
The birds showed lots of fear,
They quickly flew away
'Cause they knew the cat was there.

When squirrels came to eat the seeds
The birds did not seem scared,
They simply ate their tasty lunch
And birds and squirrels shared.

How can the birds tell who's who?
How can the birds decide
Whether they should eat the seeds,
Or fly away and hide?

I don't know the answer
And I can't really say
If a bird knows what it's doing
When it behaves that way.

Birds know that squirrels are not cats
And birds do not show fear,
Can it be that birds can think
And know when danger's near?

Snow

Do you know about snow?
It falls from the sky, you know,
It covers everything in sight,
A blanket white as white is white,
It surely is a pretty sight.

A fluffy pillow in the sky
Spills its feathers from on high,
And all the flakes come floating down
And cover all that's in our town.

I love to watch the snowflakes fall,
I'd like to try to catch them all,
And every flake is special too,
Its shape is something that's brand new.

I treasure every one of them,
'Cause each will never be again,
Each melts into a spot of wet
That disappears,
With no regret.

Ducks

The ducks went swimming by,
They looked so calm and slow,
But their feet were moving quickly
As they paddled from below.

They swam in icy water
But they did not seem to care,
They seemed so warm and cozy
As they swam from here somewhere.

Then suddenly one duck
Flew into the sky,
The other ducks soon followed,
'Til all were flying high.

They flew in a formation,
Each duck knew where to be,
The ducks' complex behavior
Seemed a mystery to me.

How did they fly that way?
And how did they keep warm?
What did they eat for food?
How did ducks survive a storm?

I wondered where they went?
And will the ducks come back?
I asked one duck these questions
And his answer was: QUACK!
                        QUACK!

Listen to Nature

I love the sounds of nature,
A bird, a brook, a tree,
Everything in nature
Speaks special things to me.

Nature says birds are happy,
And trees are happy too,
The brook that babbles onward
Has little else to do.

But humans often mess things up
And destroy the natural state,
Sometimes they are sorry
But sorrow comes too late.

Humans have to listen
To what nature has to say,
Otherwise their actions,
May make nature fade away.

Life is Everywhere

I overturned a rock
And saw a wondrous sight,
Creatures of all sorts
Came out into the light.

A ladybug, a sowbug,
A millipede and some ants,
I sat down on the ground
And the ants crawled up my pants.

All these creatures hustled,
There was no time to spare,
They looked for food and water
And scrambled everywhere.

I put the rock back in its place
And the creatures disappeared,
Although I had disturbed them,
They did not seem to be scared.

The lesson that I learned
Is that life is all around,
And if you don't believe me,
Lift a rock up from the ground.

The Active Rock

I found a rock the other day,
It was round and hard and grey,
I picked it up from where it lay
And thought what it could do today.

It could make some papers stay,
It could block a passageway,
It could hide some ants at play.

I gave the rock a big "Hooray,"
And then . . .
I threw the rock away.

To Step or Not to Step

The ant seemed very happy
Until I dug into the ground,
Then the ant climbed out
And wandered all around.

It seemed a bit bewildered
And did not know what to do,
It ran right toward my foot
And went underneath my shoe.

That posed a major problem
I had to solve real fast,
Should I step down with my shoe?
Or should I allow the ant to last?

Please help me to decide
While the ant is still in view,
To step or not to step?
What do you think I should do?

You Can Write Poems Too

eggs O O O O O O

eggs are very pretty,
they are round and white,
they have a shell around them
that is a pretty sight,
I can eat them for breakfast,
I can eat them for lunch,
dont eat the shell,
or your teeth will go crunch

(by Aaron (age 7) and marvin
Druger)

105

A taxi by Aaron Druger

I was going some where
in a city. I did not
know where to go. I
saw a yellow taxi and
it was going slow. Then
I raised my hand and
then the taxi stopped.
The taxi driver opened the
door and into it I hopped.
And to the store I shopped.

The Library Book
by Keith Jamieson (age 11)

A single book sits on the library shelf
Waiting and waiting all by itself
Knowing and knowing without a doubt
That someone will come to check it out.

The door opens wide, a young girl steps in
Checking books that are fat and books that are thin
Until she comes to our book all by itself
Waiting alone on the library shelf.

The librarian checks it out like that
Marking the book with a purple thumbtack
And the little girl skips to a gnarled oak tree
Knowing she found a good book to read.

(I asked Keith why the last line doesn't rhyme. He replied: "I got tired.")

Circles

A circle has no ending,
It has no beginning too,
If I run around in circles
I end up nowhere new.

Circles have no bottom,
Circles have no top,
If you want to find an ending,
There is no place you can stop.

Circles last forever,
They never seem to quit,
But this poem is not a circle,
It has an end . . . and this is it!

THE END

This is not really the end of this book. Poetry is endless. So, write your own poems and add them to the book.

YouR PoeMs